What's in the
Dirt?

by Martha E. H. Rustad

CAPSTONE PRESS
a capstone imprint

Little Pebble is published by Capstone Press,
1710 Roe Crest Drive, North Mankato, Minnesota 56003
www.capstonepub.com

Library of Congress Cataloging-in-Publication Data
Rustad, Martha E. H. (Martha Elizabeth Hillman), 1975– author.
 What's in the dirt? / by Martha E. H. Rustad.
 pages cm.—(Little pebble. What's in there?)
 Summary: "Simple nonfiction text and full-color photographs present animals
and plants found in soil"—Provided by the publisher.
Audience: Ages 5–7 Audience: K to grade 3
Includes bibliographical references and index.
 ISBN 978-1-4914-6012-2 (library binding)—ISBN 978-1-4914-6024-5 (pbk.)—
 ISBN 978-1-4914-6036-8 (ebook pdf)
1. Burrowing animals—Juvenile literature. 2. Soil invertebrates—Juvenile literature.
3. Soil ecology—Juvenile literature. I. Title. II. Title: What is in the dirt.
 QL756.15.R87 2016
 591.75′7—dc23   2015001935

For Walter and Maggie   MEHR

Table of Contents

Dig and Peek!

Dig a hole.

Peek underground!

What lives in the dirt?

Plants

Roots hold plants in dirt.

roots

We eat some roots.

Dig up carrots.

Look at these potatoes!

Animals

Squirm!

Worms tunnel in soil.

They eat dead plants

and dirt.

11

Ants dig a nest.

Ants live together

in groups called colonies.

13

Tarantulas hide.

Quick!

Grab a bug to eat.

15

Dig!

Moles tunnel.

Hairs on their nose

help them feel.

This owl lives in
a burrow.
It catches food
with its claws.

Bark! A prairie dog warns others. They stay safe in burrows.

Dirt makes a good home.

Glossary

burrow—an underground home

colony—a group of animals that lives together

prey—an animal that is eaten as food

root—a plant part that grows under the soil and sucks up water

Read More

Messner, Kate. *Up in the Garden and Down in the Dirt.* San Francisco: Chronicle Books, 2015.

Royston, Angela. *Animals that Dig.* Chicago: Capstone Raintree, 2014.

Internet Sites

FactHound offers a safe, fun way to find Internet sites related to this book. All of the sites on FactHound have been researched by our staff.

Here's all you do:
Visit *www.facthound.com*
Type in this code: 9781491460122

 Check out projects, games and lots more at
www.capstonekids.com

Index